BOA
EDITIONS LTD

THE HANDS OF STRANGERS
POEMS FROM THE NURSING HOME

THE HANDS OF STRANGERS

POEMS FROM THE NURSING HOME

JANICE N. HARRINGTON

AMERICAN POETS CONTINUUM SERIES, No. 130

BOA EDITIONS, LTD.   ROCHESTER, NY   2011

First Edition
11 12 13 14   7 6 5 4 3 2 1

For information about permission to reuse any material from this book please contact The Permissions Company at www.permissionscompany.com or e-mail permdude@eclipse.net.

Publications by BOA Editions, Ltd.—a not-for-profit corporation under section 501 (c) (3) of the United States Internal Revenue Code—are made possible with funds from a variety of sources, including public funds from the New York State Council on the Arts, a state agency; the Literature Program of the National Endowment for the Arts; the County of Monroe, NY; the Lannan Foundation for support of the Lannan Translations Selection Series; the Sonia Raiziss Giop Charitable Foundation; the Mary S. Mulligan Charitable Trust; the Rochester Area Community Foundation; the Arts & Cultural Council for Greater Rochester; the Steeple-Jack Fund; the Ames-Amzalak Memorial Trust in memory of Henry Ames, Semon Amzalak and Dan Amzalak; and contributions from many individuals nationwide. See Colophon on page 80 for special individual acknowledgments.

Cover Design: Sandy Knight
Cover Photo: "Windsor Park Nursing Home" courtesy Gottscho-Schleisner, Inc.
Interior Design and Composition: Richard Foerster
Manufacturing: McNaughton & Gunn
BOA Logo: Mirko

Library of Congress Cataloging-in-Publication Data

Harrington, Janice N.
  The hands of strangers : poems from the nursing home / Janice N. Harrington. — 1st ed.
    p. cm. — (American poets continuum series ; no. 130)
  ISBN 978-1-934414-54-5
  I. Title.
  PS3608.A7817H36 2011
  811'.6—dc22

                    2011001431

NATIONAL
ENDOWMENT
FOR THE ARTS
A great nation
deserves great art.

BOA Editions, Ltd.
250 North Goodman Street, Suite 306
Rochester, NY 14607
www.boaeditions.org
A. Poulin, Jr., Founder (1938–1996)

State of the Arts

NYSCA

CONTENTS

For my beloved, my heart, and my life, R.D.P.

I

IN THEIR CARE

BEDCHECKS

How quiet they breathe, the little children in their cradles.
—Walt Whitman, "The Sleepers"

3:00 a.m.

Hunched small beneath cotton blankets, curled behind metal
guards they sleep at last. The barber sleeps and dreams of nicks
and razors.

The bus driver sleeps and the cow-hipped bearer of thirteen
children sleeps. The porter sleeps in the room with the birth
defect. The Huntington's chorea sleeps on her padded floor.
The teacher, the painter of greeting cards, the one-legged vet,
all sleep.

The farm widow dreams of silos and seven gaunt and skinny cows
swallowing seven sleek and fatted cows.

The woman beaten for years by her husband finally sleeps.

The dementia sleeps and wakes, sleeps and listens for a ship,
hearing its sails and querulous gulls.

But it is only the chattering of our laundry carts, the scuff of our
crepe soles moving from room to room as we go and slowly
go—handmaids, vestals, novices—into the ward to bless each
sleeper in turn.

O *"how quiet they breathe, the little children in their cradles,"* how easily they
dream and prefer dreaming.

Let nothing disturb them, not the bedpan, not a shifting sheet,
not our steps, not our mumbled talk, not the towels folded
and unfolded, not the soap, not the running water, not pills
toppling into a paper cup, not the water pitcher or its melting
ice,

not the traffic on L street, not the dawn coming through wards of
light—the dawn coming through concussions of light beneath a
wounded sky.

Let them sleep.

BALANCE

In the night, we listened for breath,
nostrils flared for the sting of urine, or worse.
We shoved laundry carts draped with linen,
gowns, and towels, passing the sleepers by,
stepping into the rooms and beside the beds
of dreamers with disloyal bladders.

If their sheets were wet, we changed them,
washing their flanks with tepid water, adding
lotion or not, sprinkling their haunches with talc
or not, relieved if only one sheet were soiled.
We rolled the body from side to side, changing
one half of the bed, then the other, tightening
the half sheet and spreading the absorbing paper
square backed with blue plastic.

If they lay in soil, if their beds were soaked,
we hoisted them into a chair or slanted them
on a mattress seam to wait, to tremble, to catch
their breath at each uncertain move, unsteady
and fearful. Braced against indifferent bodies,
they whimpered "I'm sorry, I'm sorry,"
or tied their arms about our waists and held on.

MOLLY

Unlike the others, with her it was never rough
or quick, or half-done, and never,
because it was endless, done with anger
or jaws grinding *enough, enough.*

It was done carefully, spreading thighs,
lifting the scrotum with its rope
of penis, the leaves of labia eased aside,
a washcloth, slicked with soap,
washing flesh and flank in a tide

of heat
      of touch
            of water.

This was intimacy,
a shame they couldn't hide, but did it matter?
Handmaid, menial, servant, daughter,
each movement precise, each movement ceremony,
cradling these white-fleshed raku,
    each holding its fill of bitter tea.

All the exquisite parts of her work—fingers,
palms, wrists, arms, shoulders—
intent on the motions of cleaning and drying,
the certainty that one day she too will lie waiting
in a county bed seeking compassion
from the hands of strangers.

WHITE SLIPS

She remembers them, the old women,
    good immigrant stock,
their slips as white as altar cloth starched
sharp enough to cut, their drawers of white
cotton slips folded and pressed and creased.
    Oh, how they loved order.

She recalls the plaited hair and braids wound
into labyrinths, the greasy silk combed
and combed in slowing strokes, the solemn
sweep of hand and arm stroking those white
heads, stroking until they were girls again.
She did that for them when there was time.

Beneath her fingers they found their way
home, the old tongue returning
like a prodigal son, the ghost of a brother
lost to war, a husband to cancer.

But it was *Scheiße* when rough hands hurt
them and *Schwärze!* to the aide who lifted
them, and *mein Gott, mein Gott* the woe
they sang from wheelchair to bed.

Sharp syllables never forgotten and worn as close
to the skin as a cotton slip. *Scheiße. Schwärze.*
The words came and they cradled them:
Ja, mein Gott, mein Gott, mein Gott.

Mein Vater in Himmel. White cotton slips,
fierce perfections held against their skin

like penance, the fruit of lye soap
and Argo Laundry Starch, signs
of rectitude lifted and shaken loose
by dark-fingered *Schwärze* who care
    nothing. *O mein Gott.*

THE NIGHT-SHIFT ROSE

She begins her grooming while
her children sleep and her husband's
snores sharpen into whistles.
She stands before a full-length mirror,
freeing her hair from plastic curlers,
brushing its length and sweeping
the strands into the swell of a French roll
secured with hair spray, bobby pins,
and the precisions of a rat-tailed comb.

She smooths powder on each cheek,
reddens her lips, and presses them
firmly against a folded tissue to make
six red petals, the three long vowels
or three perfect kisses that she
will give to no one. Swiftly, she brushes
her cheekbones into blush, arches
her brows, and completes the ritual
of dampening neck, wrists, brow,
and hair in a cumulus of scent: *Tabu,
Opium, Shalimar, White Shoulders,
Charlie,* or *Cinnabar.* Already weary,

she steps back to consider the careful
reflection, a nursing home aide
leaving for work—a white uniform, white
shoes, white stockings—lifting
her keys and stepping into darkness.

Her leaving drifts over her children's heads
and enters their dreaming, the attar

of a night-shift rose, the flower favored
by moonlight, opened by sweat, and forced
by fatigue into blossom. The flower
whose only thorn is loss—O how it pricks.
O its scent upon their skin.

Always her children confuse absence
with eau de cologne. All their lives
they search for the flower that once
bloomed in their night. They test the air
after each departure, standing in darkened
rooms to stare at the blossoming moon,
so far away, petals they can never touch.

OLD PHOTOS

They never looked like their snapshots,
the days when they were young and jaunty,
with tapering calves and extraordinary hats
when someone's box camera surprised them:
arms linked around another's waist
or straddling a child on a lifted hip, caught
almost smiling or ankles-crossed before
the new Chevrolet or a red-brick bungalow.

You wouldn't know that the hand-tinted smile
belonged to this wheel-chaired denizen
hunched in her housedress with a securely
buttoned sweater and putty-colored hose.

But sometimes, an aide would stay to comb
the snow of hair, grooming an old head
with smooth, unhurried strokes, the comb's teeth
gentled downward, a meditation from brow
to nape, nape to shoulder, shoulder to back,
reveling in an old woman's hair, yellow-white
as marrow or soap, carefully roping a plait,
winding its coil, and lifting the hair between open
palms like wings or reins or the folds of a letter.

A stranger's fingers against an aging scalp,
a stranger who hefts a braid's weight to weave
a ladder, or bell rope, or sounding line.

An aide twists and binds a scrim of hair,
her attention stayed by the shallow stroking
of a plastic comb, seduced by length
and touch and muted song: Shh. Shh.

Shh. The old woman indulges the gentle tugs,
the prickings of hairpins tucked into place, holding
her head still beneath the fingers' reach, ignoring the old
photos, dusty snapshots on a nursing home dresser.

PRECISION

Two backs, two breaths, one motion,
muscles steeled to hoist and heave,
two precisions assigned the hardest ward.

Two aides, their arms cradling clean linen,
move exact as time clocks, stopping at each room
to read the odors or lack of odors, to listen
for breath, for the crack of stiff bones
or the grunted, "Nurse," their dark hands
lifting settled hips and compassing them
anew. No wasted motion. No spillage
of time or strength. No stopping.

Efficiency too is loveliness, is mercy.
The sheet smoothed beneath a naked haunch,
the soap rinsed, the ailing joint seamlessly
shifted and eased by practiced gestures
and diligence are also grace.

Doing the job because it must be done,
by room, by bed, by measure, by ccs in
or ccs out, repeatedly and to schedule—
that too is weight, weight they carried,

the two of them never slacking, always
the hardest ward, working together
for years, no one faster, no one better.
Two backs, two breaths, one motion.

PIETÀ

She stoops, this should-have-retired
aide, in her polished and re-polished
shoes and white uniform, lifting
this fetaled shape, the body
of a wordless man who only groans,
his eyes startled into clear ice.

His blue-milk skin, blue-veined
and blue-bruised, eases against her chest.
His brow leans into her shoulder. His lips
press her uniform's rough pleats and leave

damp wings traced in spittle above her breast,
though she does not notice and, straining,
bears the weight as the years have taught,
her knees bent, back levered into straightness,
breathing in, breathing out, muscles tight.
She lowers him as you would lower an over-
filled basin, settling its shallow wash gently,
leaving even the refracted light undisturbed.

WARDS OF SLEEP

How soft the soles of aides at night, how
quietly they slip from breath to breath,
lifting waste and weight and waiting through
the hours till morn, weary for home
and wards of sleep, where dreams
arise with stethoscopes and white uniforms.

How low and slumped and shapeless
the woman who waits in her wheelchair
after breakfast, lifting her head
at each approaching step to stare,
like the owner of a sold house gazing
into empty rooms before softly shutting the door.

How still, how still, lies a man when he is dead,
when an aide washes him for the last time,
face, belly, limbs, groin, and back,
steeping her cloth in soap-gray water
and wringing it dry again, urging the lather
across cooling skin, though only the cloth,
only her sleeves and dampened cuffs, only
the muscles of her back and her breath move.

How empty the bed that held someone once
for a year, for two, for five or more,
how taut its sheets, how severe its seams'
geometry. How patiently a bed waits
with linens stripped, mattress turned,
its frame newly steamed, with metal railings
wrenched hard into place and locked.

II

WARDS

ROT

This little piggy cried wee wee wee
all the way home

We cared for her and watched the furious streaks,
the flesh gone yellow, gray-green, then black,
the darkness creeping from toe to toe, from toe to arch,
till through the ruptured skin we could see her graying
muscle. We could see her bones. But we turned
her every hour, as the nurses directed, turned her
gingerly so as not to lose the softened flesh.
We lifted the ruined foot, wrapped in a paper layer,
and eased it into a garbage bag to catch its leaking.
That the bag was airless, a plastic kiln for already
burning flesh, we did not consider, doing the best
we could, doing what the nurses told us, giving
her codeine with sips of water, watching
as her urine darkened. But it didn't matter.

She slept mostly, moaning when we lifted her head
to press a cup against her lips, moaning as we turned
her. Each day, the nurse begged her family: *Reconsider,*
please reconsider. How many days? How many hours?
Enough for the foot to fall from the ankle, for the Achilles'
string to slacken, rotted through, for us to reel away,
dizzied by wretchedness, afraid that we would watch
the gangrenous blackening from ankle to calf.
But at last the nurse called enough times. The son's
wife came. She went in and hurried out, saying *Oh.*
Oh, we didn't know. And we hated them.

LEGS

First the toes, then the feet,
then the calves below
the knee—just stubs,

that was all (after the third
operation) she had left,

brown stubs she rubbed
when the weather changed,

rubbed
while she waited in the hall,
or sat the hours in a wheelchair.

The aides hoisted her atop foam
or sheep's skin, lifted her half-body
like a clapperless bell, and wondered
at the slow pruning, slow paring
away of a woman's body,
how suffering shaved so little
from the ability to suffer.

She rubbed her once-legs
between brown fists, rolling the flesh
as if to erase the little she had left.

TWO

Ugly as a fifty-cent housedress
in a thrift store bargain bin, or canker sores,
or the gray-white writhings beneath
a seam of mulch, or the rain-beat cat
skulked down beneath the dumpster's shadow—that ugly,

and yet, one
will help the other into her wheelchair,
struggle pastel sleeves stained with dried yolk
over the hunched shoulders, brush the wisps
and stalks of hair, blush mottled cheeks
and limn scant lips *wet cherry red* or *apricot glow.*
Afterward, squeezing the wheelchair's
handles, the one who is still limber will push
both chair and invalid to the dining room. One

will pat the other's hand, and the other
will rub a soothing palm over a knob
of shoulder. Each hand trembles,
clumsy with stiffness: yellow roots
knotted with bruised veins.

Sitting before a plastic tray, one
feeds the other and wipes
the slobbered jowl with a tissue
tucked between sleeve and wrist.
Cooed and petitioned, one smacks
and sputters and sucks, spoon
by spoon, mouth open—little parrot,
little hatchling. She swallows every drop,
every scraping, though not the coffee,

which is bitter, and the one holding
the spoon, a remnant of the generation
that never wastes or forgets hunger, slips
a fold of bread into her sagging pocket.
For later, she says, but she forgets, and after a day
or two she is surprised to see the hard crusts,
the grit that falls from her pocket, a trail
for what will find them yet. Two old women.

STARCH

For Donna

She was the human plank,

the slab, the level we lifted and lowered, hinging her narrow length
on and off the bedpan, sponging the skin and removing the gown
that sheltered a child's drawing: stick arms, stick legs, a crayon-
black triangle of hair.

We dressed her in her gingham gowns, gowns with ribbons or
delicate buttons, gowns splayed across atrophied muscle like a
gingham bell ringing the handiwork of a diligent seamstress.

But it was not the hem's tolling, not the empty pockets, not the
pearl-dotted buttons that made her grieve but her flat and deflated
sleeves. She complained, complained, complained until, coaxing and
cussing beneath our breaths, we pinched the folds into pinnacles,
into starchy cathedrals and stiff meringues.

Indurate, rigid, and rock, a woman who could move only her eyes
and the tipmost knuckle of a still-pliant joint, she pulled the string
that kindled the light, the light that drew us back to arthritic words
pushed through a fence of teeth: *fix the sleeves.* We preened and
pricked the sullen folds, bulged planes into globes, until at last, like
her sleeves, we were schooled and shaped, billowing the cloth into
lanterns and lungs of air, into cumulus and gingham balloons that
rose and dragged behind their useless strings.

VISITS

Thumb to index, thumb to middle,
thumb to ring, thumb to pinky,

all day the same motion.

Thumb to index, thumb to middle,
thumb to ring, thumb to pinky.

Alma worked her fingers, one against the other, whispering
something about a boy, something about "He." Bits of words and
phrases floated from her mouth like dust. If you spoke to her,
"Good morning, Alma," she'd say "Yeah yeah." No matter what
you said to her, "Yeah yeah," then laughter. Every day we dressed
her, urged her to sit on the commode, and wiped her, then coaxed
her to the dining room where we wheedled spoons of mash between
her lips and returned her to the mustard-colored chair where she
spent her days, her fingers tapping one against the other.

Thumb to index, thumb to middle,
thumb to ring, thumb to pinky.

The chart said he beat her. A long marriage that left her brain-
damaged. He didn't visit often. But you could tell when he had
sat beside her chair and covered her busy fingers with his own.
Afterwards, she wandered in any direction, her patter a muttered
rush, something about a boy and something about "He." She shook
and whipped her fingers like loose keys, shaking them back and
forth, as if to sign an unknown and difficult language.

REALITY ORIENTATION THERAPY

To orient the elderly who may become confused, upon awakening them tell them the time of day, identify the nursing home, use their names and the name of the current president.

—Instructions for new aides

Scree! Scree! The starling's soliloquy. Was that this morning? No, starlings have no songs. They cough like old men. The bed is on fire. The starlings come bearing the news, metal voices—knives, forks. Is that my name? No one knows my hair was once the purple black of a starling's wing. A knife calls my name again. Precedent? Yes, there might be precedent, but it's only Monday. In the hallway, I see ten thousand starlings. Wings, wings, so bright everyone is blinded. See, the bed is on fire. My skin burns. The fork pokes the air again. The knife cuts. A present? The present? The fork has a lisp. But my hands are empty. My fingers unwrap the flames, unfold them. Inside there are wings. The fork wraps its prongs around my shoulders and lifts me, ignoring the flames, ignoring the wings. The knife repeats *Scree! Scree!* The starling's soliloquy—have they come to take me home?

WALKING ROBA

Along the bases and linoleum
of the county home,
           she walked Roba,
old batter in the Negro Leagues,
the two of them, aide and elder,
moving slowly down the ward
to the dining room.

His bladder urgent,
and his own door too far away,
they stepped into a room like any other,
county owned, county given,
and in a county chair
a Salt Lake City barber
lifted the razor of his tongue.

Get that nigger out of here.
You can't bring that nigger in here.

Roba stopped
as if the words crossed an infield
where his mind stretched
to catch their meaning.

Come on, Roba. Come on,
and she walked him to another room,
helped him wrestle pants and suspenders.

Roba's mind, at last,
wrenched itself
from confusion:

Cracker!

Piss hit the side of the bowl
in a hard satisfying stream.

They walked on, aide and elder,
knowing the way, the doors open
to them, the doors closed.
The aide said nothing.
A shift, a workday, nearly done.

MAY ENGLES

*May Engles died yesterday. No family, no friends, no possessions, just
a room provided by the county, no pastor, no nurses, no anything. No
book will ever give her a sentence.*

—Aide's diary, Aug. 11, 1977

May Engles died and she died of scurvy.
May Engles died and she died of sorrow.
May Engles died and she died like this, *oh-oh, oh-oh.*
May Engles died or maybe she didn't.

Tomorrow, ring bells, burn effigies of crones. Declare it May Engles
    Day.
Let mothers name their babies May or Engles.
Let astrologers re-name Orion's Belt and call it May Engles' garter.
Let believers see her face on mildewed wallpaper in a Day's Inn in
    Biloxi.
Let biologists name a newly discovered orchid May Engles, or a
    moth, or a deep-sea squid not seen since the Pliocene era.
Let poets write in the form of May Engles: small and plain and
    common.

May you travel with thirty other pilgrims to find her grave, but
    not finding it, may you open a boutique to sell May Engles
    memorabilia and sack lunches to tourists who want to lie in the
    county bed where May Engles died.
May you live out your days as happy as May Engles.

May you whisper, before pressing your tongue against the slope of
    your beloved's neck, *May Engles, O May Engles.*

May Engles plucked the feathers of the last Lord God Bird. She is
    the nude on the far right in Cézanne's *Les Grandes Baigneuses.*

Yesterday, anthropologists discovered the image of a small woman
  leaping amidst a herd of antelope at Lascaux. They have called
  her May Engles.

May Engles has seven overdue library books.
Below your right kidney, the doctor will find proof of May Engles.
  Yes, you are in good health.

On a playground in Alabama, black girls clap their hands.
  They've made a rhyme for May Engles:

Ol' May Engles   *Engles!*
Looks like shingles   *Engles!*
Her bones go jingle   *Engles!*
Her toenails tingle   *Engles!*

Your daddy stole a puddin'   *Engles!*
He made your mama cry   *Engles!*

Now they gonna hang 'em on the Fourth of July.

The water laps—May and May—against the shore. The earth
  answers, and the wind, and the boy swinging his toes above the
  dock, all with the same glad syllable: May and May and May.

Afterward, the boy will snatch a fish from the dark water. He'll
  split its belly and find a golden ring. Lifting the ring, he'll cry,
  "May Engles!"

Some say
  a small woman now stands beside Death. She touches those
  whom Death chooses. She lifts the dead from their tangled
  veins, as if their bodies were beds they lay in for too long.

Some say

that before dying, if you whisper the woman's name, Death will slow, surprised that you remember a woman without family or monument or possession. Death will slow, and you will have a moment, and maybe—another moment—more.

May Engles,

May Engles,

May Engles.

THE WAY IT ENDS

Amidst a ward of schizophrenics, strokes,
Parkinson sufferers, birth defects, colostomies,
radiation burns, heart disease, psoriasis,
diabetes, cancer, syphilis, Huntington's chorea,
hunting accidents, dementias, arthritics,
amputations, cataracts, mastectomies,
retardations, depressions, blindness—this:

an old married couple, admitted together.

Both invalid, and yet she watched him
as a mother coddles her child's first steps
up the school stair. She watched, weighing
their effort, doing what the aides have left
undone. She soothed his patchy hair, locked
the buttons of his sweater, swabbed
the gummy matter from his eyes, and erased
the sluggish tracks of spittle. *There now.*
There we are. Now, that's better isn't it?
That's my fella. That's my boy. Though
he did no more than nod and seep
a thready drool. At night, the aides rolled

their beds together. He lay curled, asleep,
while she attended, stretching thin arms
through the bedrails to snug his blankets
and kiss her fingers against his cheek.
Later, waking, she called the aides,
worried that his bed was soiled, that his
blanket was not enough and not tucked
correctly. *Are his feet cold?* she asked.

He shouldn't be cold—or once calling
because she had soaked his sheets trying
to tend his dry lips with a plastic cup.
The story ends, as you know it will,
one died before the other.

III

ROUGH HANDS

PROTEST

There is a way to drop a body atop a hard mattress,
to scrub gentle parts too hard, to yank a gown
across withered flesh, to drag a weight smaller
than your own and slam it against a pillow.
There are ways to say the night is long
and there are twenty other beds to check.

There are ways to ignore chapping lips,
not to hear a rasping voice, to avoid the task
of filling a water pitcher. There are ways
to tell them, without using words, that you hate
the job, ways to leave them cold and shivering
and naked. There are ways to leave them alone.

But they had an answer, the ones we cleaned
and dressed and moved and fed and watched
over. On chair, bed, pillow, gown, on sheet,
diaper, floor, and shoe, writ repeatedly
in stinking letters: No, I am not dead.

MENDING WALL

Never carefully enough, never slowly
enough are old women lifted and lowered
into their rolling chairs. Scraped, scratched,
pierced by roughness, old women split

as easily as sun-scalded plums: torn
by uniform buttons, the loose buckle
of a flopping restraint, fingernails,
watchbands, a wedding ring's silver setting,

and a washcloth's coarse nudgings.
Nurses' aides are friction. A ward
is a serrated edge. Injured, the skin parts:
four tears on one arm, scabs, and white scars.

With a cotton swab, the aide prods a skin
flap back into place, gently flattening the rolled
edge, but still the wound opens, the seam seeps.
On a county ward, old women wait, holding

their mummied arms dressed with ointment
and peroxide, paper-taped and gauzed.
They learn to take the splitting skin
and seeping scabs for granted, understanding

that the body loses interest and refuses,
at last, to keep its wall. The blood slows,
the skin thins, a scratch on an old woman's arm
widens into a door. Carefully, she steps through.

FRICTION'S FLOWERS

Old age is the time of blooming,
and nursing homes flower in all seasons:
yellow tulips on an old woman's housedress,
chrysanthemum tissues tucked
into a palsied fist, and at the nurse's station
the falsely named amaryllis, bright
trumpets atop a pedestal of stalk.

From a distance, even bedsores have petals,
are calendulas, are daisies, are bed roses
embossed upon hip or buttock or shoulder,
proving that the body is bud, the skin—leaf.
The body is bloom, the skin—petal,
at least from a distance. The aide

considered none of this. The nurse's station
poinsettia did not trouble her, nor the plastic
flowers in their plastic vases. They were not
beds to make or residents to bathe, weight to lift
or mouths to fill. Yet she lifted lap robes
and laid them atop immobile legs, spread
their crocheted blossoms to hide the twiggy
legs, tucked them around waist or under
thigh the way a gardener tucks bulbs
beneath a fold of earth. She paper-taped

the skin of crones and sealed their ruptures
and avulsions, their forearms abloom with hues
of purple-red, blue-green, and green-blue,
friction's flowers, the florescence of touch
and careless bruising. From pain we also blossom;

in pain the language of all flowers, as white roses
are secrecy and silence and geraniums folly,
as lavender sings of solitude and the purple hyacinth
pleads, unanswered, *Forgive me, I am sorry.*

PINCH

In a room bright with sunlight, an aide feeds
purée to an old woman in a wheelchair.

The old woman, blinded by cataracts,
rolls the brownish mash between her lips.

The aide scrapes the woman's lips and chin
with the spoon edge and pushes the spillings

between her lips again. But the old woman
does not want to eat, or perhaps needs more time

to swallow, or perhaps does not like the brown mash,
and instead she spits. The aide spoons more mash

between her lips, and the old woman, reaching,
snatches the skin on the aide's bare arm

and squeezes its fold hard between two
rooty fingers, smiling. She thinks, by this small

violence, that she has won, that she is the victor
of the contest, not to be ignored, not defenseless.

But *this* aide pinches her back: fierce and sharp.
The old woman widens opaque eyes,

straining to see this scorpion, this scissor-beaked
bird, this awl and mirror image—this enemy,

but in her eyes are cloud banks, splinters
of dazzle, and shadow. She sees nothing

and feels pinpricks, ice, broken glass,
and hate, hate, hate. They spar, pinch for pinch,

until the eyes draw their curtains, until at last
there comes a cry that no one hears but the aide,

who takes the tray and taps the spoon
against the glass and clears the puréed splatter.

Whatever is uneaten remains so.
Whatever hungers goes unfed.

WIND

I an old man,
A dull head among windy spaces.
—T. S. Eliot, "Gerontion"

The aides come with their hands of wind,
in their white uniforms, white winds,
a white sirocco to scour our dry skins.

Their voices are voices of wind,
low, mean winds that hurl in alleys
and toss the greasy news overhead.

Pull your collar against it, duck
your head, and still the splinter
finds your eye. The girls come with
their windy ways, the wind in their
arms and legs, the wind

that snatches the covers back
and blows away sleep's topsoil, wind
that drags you from curled warmth,
as if a garbage can lumbered down
the street, voices

of wind that you hear in the hall,
not storms, not breezes, but sighs
that do no more than push stenches
from here to there. Though out there,

in the space you left behind, there
is also wind. You hear it. Eyes pressed
to the pane, you see it, strong wind

that thrashes the trees and makes them bend,
loud and sea-sounding, but maybe
angry only because it is not that vast,
or deep, or measureless, only wind

that comes and goes, torments
some flying thing—halting
it in midair—tearing the flight
from its wings.

GENTLY

He lays her down upon the bed,
unsnaps the housedress
with its pockets bulged with tissue,

unrolls the sausage socks
from her thin legs, knotted with veins,
and pulls the flimsy panties

with their sad elastic downward.
She hits his hands, slaps them.
He the aide and she the resident,

the *room*, that he readies for bed.
Confused, she tries to rise, tries
to pull the housedress back over

her withered breast, but he snatches it.
She says o three times, vowels
as small as peppermints o o

o. He tells her *hush* and lifts
her flaccid breasts and drops them
like the door latches to empty rooms,

and undoes the buckle to his belt,
and undoes the belt, and draws
the zipper low, and lowers his pants,

and climbs on top of her. O o o
she says more frantic than before
but he covers her mouth. o.

The strand of hair against his face
he brushes away. Her gray hair.
No one sees it fall.

FEET

They gripped his calves and swung him
from bed to seat in one swift stroke.
With one hand, he grabbed the mattress edge
and with the other fumbled for their shoulders.
Careful, careful, he said.

His feet, crooked planks, jutted
into the air, deformed by cheap leather
and unfortunate genes—the toes beveled
inward, pinched to a shoe-shaped point,
an open crater on the knot of each big toe.

They choked his feet into trouser socks, yanked
corduroy slippers into place, and drew him up
to mince and halt his way along the hall.
Careful, careful, he said.

Afterwards, between rush and schedule,
they slid and dragged him to his room,
a high-stepping marionette snatching
wounded feet and dropping them down again,
pulled by the aides' relentless steps,

a once-upon-a-time hotel porter staring
until his face darkened, but never speaking,
as if words were patent-leather shoes on Sunday
morning, tight and pinching, shoes that took you
nowhere comfortably and were mostly show.

Girls just doing the job. They didn't know
that a sheet's weight could break a man, could make

him moan, didn't know the blues that linger
in a man's feet when he sleeps in a county bed.
They never knew, and all he said was *Careful, careful.*

ARMISTICE

In the evening, they gather for Spades
or Pitch. They pass time and tell stories
about drought and dust, about farmhands
shuffled from harvest to harvest,
about the years after the war.

They suck curling smoke and bitter
coffee, slap aces and splay winnings.
The game's music is the snatch
and flick of cards, the soft *pah-aaaah*
of exhaled breaths, the *ka-crik*
of stiff knuckles. Later,

after Delia's baby doll is laid aside, after
Patsy's hips are powdered and a dry
washcloth pushed between her thighs,
after Ray is turned and all the tremblers,
wheelchaired feeble, and palsied infirm
put down, the aides will take their breaks
beside the card players. The game

will start anew, and the sons of farmers
and farmhands, the sons of elevator workers
and well-diggers, tender their lessons—
Spades, Poker, Five Card Draw, Skat,
Rummy, Spit—they finger the deck
and shuck the greasy suits into practiced
palms, smiling only as they take the trick
or lay the ace in a sigh of smoke,
always unbeatable. The aides—

the immigrant, the one released
from reform school, the one without
a father, the one with a pulled shoulder,
the one who works the kitchen and drops
cigarette ash into the oatmeal, the one
who blows smoke up her baby's nose,
these aides play and laugh—*Don't you do it!*
Don't you pull trump—laugh and watch
their chances slapped away by callused
palms. The aides deal or watch or root,

schooled by old men who have already
taught them to draw a straight-edge slow,
slow, and upward over a soaped skin,
to kindle a match against a tarry nail,
to gentle down the yeast-gummied hoods
of foreskins to wash the hidden
pulp—useful lessons—and especially
this art of shuffling cards in a seamless
motion like hands clapping or a flock
of doves released after the treaty is signed.

IV

ALL THINGS LABOR

PRESSURE WOUNDS

Blood trench, meat sump,
Devil's kiss,
sleep rot, flesh blow,
bed rose, maggot well,
old man's teacup,

peine forte et dure,
Where-Death-Has-Dined,
pus pit, grave pinch,
mattress canker,
Satan's ear,
a bed's blessing,
a bed's curse,

At-Night-the-Flesh-Is-Eaten,
bed crater, bed gall, bed pox,
skin erosion, skin decay,
friction's flower, pus purse,
the body's betrayal,

decubital gangrene,
bed rest injury,
invalid's bane, skin ulcer,
pressure sore,
necrosis, necrotic lesion,
All-Flesh-Is-Burden,
There-Are-Insatiable-Gods.

CATHETER

Its vinyl tube insinuated
between intimacies, between gapping

thighs and labia, between
vagina and anus, into

the urethra. A rubber hose, dangling,
bladder to bladder, leaking

acid and waste, drop,
and particular, drop.

This conversation between
self and polymerized, vinyl acetate,

the difference between
this reservoir and this reservoir dangling

its bulb, a swollen tumor.

Cut it. Deflated, the tube loosens, slithers,
bearing its forbidden knowledge:

we are water and salt, saline seas.
Our words, our meaning spill

and spill, sour and strong-smelling,
bitter because we have not thirsted enough.

The world awash in glory and we swallow
only the smallest drops. Cut it

and fall again, cast out or unable to bear
the irritation: that we are

vulnerable and always open, that we cannot close
even this small part of ourselves:

this tube, its itch and invasion, its gravity.
Pull, bear the pain, bear the wrenched

open agony. Freedom hurts, yes!
Pull. It will come, with blood, with pus,

with amber urine. This tube, rope,
tongue, clapper, this plastic

calligraphy still dangling
our resolve to be separate.

IMPACTION

Wear latex gloves.
The resident can stand, legs
straddled, or curl in bed to one side.

Spread K-Y over gloved fingers.
Push one digit into the anus.
The sphincter will tighten,
but the muscles will give. Move past, push,
probe. You'll feel it,
a hard mass or rounded pebbles:
what you'll pry and pull free,
what you'll remove.

Push on the stomach, dig it out,
green-lumped, tarry clinging:
turn your nose away.
They may groan. Their hands
may swat and slap, but mostly
they suffer what has to be done.

Use two fingers, push hard.
Do the job, probe, pull, but be careful.
The nurses won't tell you. No one warns
you that flesh walls tear, that the body's
boundaries wear away.

No one tells you about the red bright flow,
the serpent that slides from her anus
or about you—with two fangs thrust
up, hissing. Shhhhhhh.

ODE TO THE BEDPAN

Consider the arching hips, the buttocks
squeezed, thrust upward and then pressed
to that metal lip, almost sexually. Consider
the bedpan—shit bucket, night bowl, hat—
its adaptable demeanor: saddled, slipper-shaped,
sloped, enameled, plastic, antique porcelain,
disposable, yellow to match the pitcher
and the plastic glass, spoon-colored or blue,
the faithful servant who bears away the human
ordure, its stench and its dye-free tissues. Feel
its patience. A bedpan waits more placidly
than a woman curbing her dog. Washed out,
it is used again. How many buttocks and thighs
has a bedpan cradled? How many beds has it sat upon?
The warmth of a bedpan forgotten beneath
a sleeping rump. The floor-jarring percussion
of a bedpan dropped on the night shift. Consider
its calm, its kindness, really, that a bedpan accepts
these urges, spillings, the bowel's complaining
and the voweled protest. It does the job
assigned to it. Thigh, buttock, hip, the hand
that takes it away, embarrassment—
it is all the same. Shame—yes—but
that too is easily sluiced, nothing that anyone
should keep or have to sleep with. Bedpans
do not judge us. They are a measure
of humility, a scoop, a shovel, a gutter,
a necessary plumbing, the celebrant of hierarchy
and the social order, pleased to be lifted
by darker hands paid the minimum wage.

CHART

New residents will be examined on arrival.

How to catalog an aging body?
Do you strip it? Fix its measure
with vision's caliper? Detail mole
and mottling, the scalpel's
theorems transcribed in flesh,
contusion, bruise, and tortured bone?

Do you ask, *Who has hurt you?*
Whose body have you hurt?

If there is no answer, complete the inventory:
weight, height, beats per minute, pliability,
hue, symptoms—data to shape into alibi
(the scars were there on arrival).
The thing itself: a body but old.

Record scars or injuries on the diagram provided.

At the broken places:
keloids, calluses, grafted tissue, cysts,
and hems of flesh.

Skin held too long beneath the x-ray's eye
cauliflowers into stone.

Skin seared in a fire or scalded
seeps like the walls of an old cave.

The aged have it right: leave skin behind.
Fold it up. Let it wrinkle, tear, slip away.
Shed and dander. Walk on without it.
Go only in your bones.

Describe the resident's health and responsiveness.

Eyes, distorted behind thick lenses,
blink, shift toward the door, and shift
back again. An old woman waits
half-dressed on the edge of a bed
before a girl in a white uniform.
A stethoscope snakes around the girl's
neck. Latex gloves bulge from one pocket.
A tube of K-Y or Neosporin pokes
from the other. The girl's eyes skim over
the old woman's body. She scratches
a printed form with a ballpoint pen.
We're going to get you checked in now.

Something to do with nakedness,
something to do with looking,
something to do with a form
in a metal binder, with the drawing
of a human body—flat, sexless,
a round oval for a face. The body
an open space except for a few scars
sketched in with crooked lines.
The old woman waits for the girl
to finish writing. She holds the thermometer—
little finger, little stick—under her tongue.
If she bites down too hard, mercury
will spill out. It will look like silver rain,

like little silver peas. The old woman smiles.
The girl records *Resident in good mood.*

Is she?

Take blood pressure.

The black lung-bulb squeezes *ush,*
ush, ushhh. The cuff does not know
its strength. It is a father's grip.
Ushhhhhh.

She thinks of her father from grip

The armband
of a fascist regime, the squeezing fist
of a lover—*don't go, don't go*—but they go,
and love goes—which raises the blood pressure.

Has she lost someone?

(Angered, the aide squeezes the bulb
fast and hard and too tight.)

The old woman says nothing. The aide
says nothing. Through the stethoscope,
the blood beats against the aide's ear.
She records a number.
The old woman rubs her arm.

Does the aide realize what may be going through the woman in mind? She should really try to deal with her focus on differently.

Record resting heart rate.

A door opens and a door closes.
A man's fist raps against a table.
The heel of a boisterous child or
a chair rocking *a-ba, a-ba* against
a wooden floor, a pounding heart
has the rhythm of a train, steel wheels

the noises of the nursing home operate to the beating of her heart. It's similar

on steel tracks. It's the dog's paw
raking the tarmac, the dog the car
struck, the dog's long whimper.
The heart is a crone with her walker
in the long ward of a nursing home—
chah, chah—a rest, a rattle—*chah,*
chah—and she starts again.

Attach information to medical history.

In every chart waits catalog, history,
and measure: fluid intake, meds given,
Rx, po, prn, qd, qid, tab, TPR, I & O,

one sentence and maybe a few more.
Words—like keys to the medications
—only in assigned hands, used only
when necessary, locked afterwards.

Complained of pain in leg. Turned regularly.
Catheter drained 10cc. Dressing changed.

Toward the back of the chart, near
its aluminum cover, a copy of an intake
sheet, a line drawing of the body,
a resident's history. *Something*, the nurse
tells the new aide, *to help you*
get to know our residents better.

In a hurried hand, what the family said
or words from an older chart. *Bus driver.*
Mother. Always made her own Christmas cards.
English teacher. Loves to crochet. Fifteen

grandkids. And then a few more words
giving the disease or medical condition,
no more than a sentence, no more
than anyone will want to remember.

[handwritten annotation:] If this is the case, is the information provided actually relevant to the woman's care or rest of the life she will live however it may be?

THE DIVIDER

Drop the thermometer in its slough.
Undo the cuff. Remove the gauze and alcohol.
Take off the stethoscope. Return the cart,
the medical chart, the syringes, and the cellophane.
Drain the humidifier. Wind the call light's string.
Scour the bedpan and the emesis basin.
Straighten the nightstand and rid the drawers
of Kleenex, buttermints, sour-apple swabs,
the false-teeth cleanser, the socks, the salves,
the ointment, and the Christmas card.
Clean the cup, the pitcher, and the tray.
Later, take the personal belongings away or
give them to someone. Strip the mattress pad
and sheets. Sterilize the bed frame's metal
skeleton. Do all this—but for now just close
its scrim around the bed, draw the divider, leave.

EPILOGUE

NECK

I will go again to Manchester Manor,
walk its wards, and lay myself down
in a cradle-bed, between parallel
rails, and wait for a girl like the girl I was,
impatient and unlearned in caring,
to loop her arms under my shoulders
and swing me to sit dizzy-spinning

against a mattress edge, my palsied hand
trembling for hers, though she will not notice.
Then, drawing breath and squeezing
her muscles taut, she will draw my body up

and drop it into a waiting chair. But I
will know to hold her neck and bear
it down, my weight pulling on that slender
column and riding it earthward, though she struggles
to turn away. Her face twists. "Let go," she says.
"Let go of me." She tries to wrench my arms away,
but I cling to that callow strength, hold
tightly to its soft meat.
    How vast am I?
My shadow can't fill a county bed.
    How permanent am I?
My sheets are removed with the twist of a wrist.
    How heavy am I?
At last! Some consequence: I am borne,
I am held and shuttled. I burden
this world even with dull gums, even
with my slow, willful enduring.
    How small am I?

Her neck answers,
the pedestal neck, the mast neck, the bell-towered neck,
its fleshy rope a spring birch.

I will swing from its bough into the day,
into a chair of chrome and vinyl
and rubberized steel, beneath a cheerful lap robe.

I will swing from her neck into flight, though
she warns me, "Never do that again.
Never hold on when I'm trying to lift you."

ACKNOWLEDGMENTS

I am grateful to the editors of the journals where some of these poems previously appeared, sometimes in earlier versions.

Crab Orchard Review: "Pinch," "Pockets," "White Slips";
Lake Effect: "Friction's Flowers";
The Mid-America Poetry Review: "Walking Roba";
New Delta Review: "May Engles";
PANK: "Balance," "Impaction," "Pietà," and "Wards of Sleep";
Quiddity: "Two," "Old Photos," "Armistice," and "Mending Wall";
Rattle: "Molly"; "Ode to the Bedpan";
Specs: "Protest," "Catheter," "Neck."

I am deeply grateful to the Rona Jaffe Foundation, whose funding gave me time to write, re-envision, and expand. I am also grateful for support from the National Endowment for the Arts Literature Fellowship for Poetry, which helped me break ground for this book.

Special thank you as well to Michael Madonick, Samira Didos, Molly MacRae, and Elizabeth Hearne.

ABOUT THE AUTHOR

Janice N. Harrington's *Even the Hollow My Body Made Is Gone* won the A. Poulin, Jr. Poetry Prize form BOA Editions and the Kate Tufts Discovery Award. She is also a Cave Canem fellow and the author of several children's books. A former librarian, she teaches creative writing at the University of Illinois.

BOA Editions, Ltd. American Poets Continuum Series

COLOPHON

The Hands of Strangers: Poems from the Nursing Home by Janice N. Harrington is set in Centaur MT, a digitalized version of the font designed for Monotype by Bruce Rogers in 1928. The italic, based on drawings by Frederic Warde, is an interpretation of the work of the sixteenth-century printer and calligrapher Ludovico degli Arrighi, after whom it is named.

The publication of this book is made possible, in part, by the special support of the following individuals:

Anonymous

Nin Andrews

Bernadette Catalana

Peter & Suzanne Durant

Charles & Naomi Erdmann

Pete & Bev French

Anne Germanacos

Suzanne Gouvernet

Robin, Hollon & Casey Hursh, *in memory of Peter Hursh*

X. J. Kennedy

Jack & Gail Langerak

Katy Lederer

Deborah Ronnen & Sherman Levey

Rosemary & Lew Lloyd

Peter & Phyllis Makuck

Michael Waters & Mihaela Moscaliuc

Boo Poulin

Cindy Winetroub Rogers

Steven O. Russell & Phyllis Rifkin-Russell

Vicki & Richard Schwartz

Ellen & David Wallack

Glenn & Helen William

Anne C. Coon & Craig J. Zicari